A·FIRST·BOOK·OF
OPPOSITES

Illustrated by David Anstey
Written by AJ Wood

MODERN PUBLISHING
A Division of Unisystems, Inc.
New York, New York 10022

HAPPY...

...SAD

DRY...

...WET

LONG...

...SHORT

CLEAN...

...DIRTY

OLD...

...NEW

HOT...

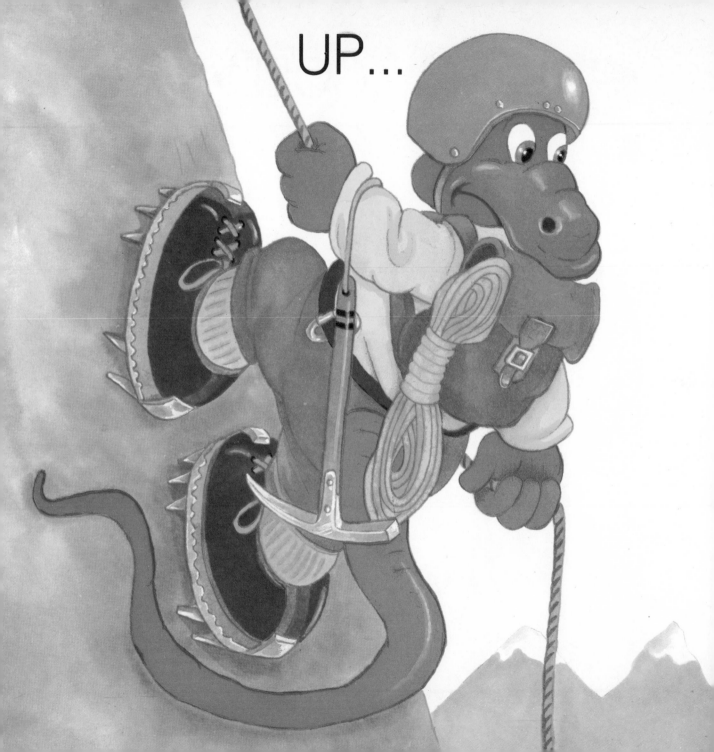

...DOWN

UNDER...

...OVER

NEAR...

PUSH...

NOISY...   ...QUIET

THE END